CW01220118

JPR WILLIAMS: IN PURSUIT OF RUGBY GLORY

Raymond J. Lipton

JPR Williams

All rights reserved.

No part of this publication may be reproduced, distributed, or transmitted in any form or by any means, including photocopying, recording, or other electronic or mechanical methods, without the prior written permission of the publisher, except in the case of brief quotations embodied in critical reviews and certain other noncommercial uses permitted by copyright law.

Copyright © Raymond J. Lipton, 2024

JPR Williams

TABLE OF CONTENTS

INTRODUCTION

CHAPTER 1: WHO IS JPR WILLIAMS
1.1 EARLY DAYS
1.2 CHILDHOOD INFLUENCES
1.3 SPORTING BEGINNINGS
1.4 PASSION FOR RUGBY AWAKENS

CHAPTER 2: RISE TO PROMINENCE
2.1 SCHOOL RUGBY DAYS
2.2 CLUB BEGINNINGS
2.3 NATIONAL RECOGNITION

CHAPTER 3: THE RED JERSEY
3.1 WALES DEBUT
3.2 INTERNATIONAL TRIUMPHS
3.3 LION TOUR SUCCESS

CHAPTER 4: THE ART OF FULLBACK PLAY
4.1 DEFENSIVE MASTERY
4.2 ATTACKING PROWESS
4.3 TACTICAL BRILLIANCE

CHAPTER 5: BEYOND THE PITCH
5.1 LIFE BEYOND RUGBY

JPR Williams

5.2 PROFESSIONAL CAREER
5.3 PERSONAL PURSUITS

CHAPTER 6: CHALLENGES AND TRIUMPHS
6.1 INJURIES
6.2 SETBACKS
6.3 MOMENTS OF TRIUMPH
6.4 LEGACY IN RUGBY

CHAPTER 7: OFF THE FIELD
7.1 INFLUENCE
7.2 LEGACY
7.3 COMMUNITY ENGAGEMENT
7.4 RETIREMENT
7.5 REFLECTION

CONCLUSION

JPR Williams

All rights reserved.

No part of this publication may be reproduced, distributed, or transmitted in any form or by any means, including photocopying, recording, or other electronic or mechanical methods, without the prior written permission of the publisher, except in the case of brief quotations embodied in critical reviews and certain other noncommercial uses permitted by copyright law.

Copyright © Raymond J. Lipton, 2024

JPR Williams

INTRODUCTION

In the completely exhilarating field of rugby, not many names reverberate with as much power and ability as JPR Williams. His excursion from humble starting points to turning into a symbol of the game is a demonstration of commitment, expertise, and a steady enthusiasm for the game. " JPR Williams: In Quest for Rugby Brilliance" disentangles the convincing story of a man whose name became inseparable from rugby significance.

Naturally introduced to a reality where rugby was something other than a game — it was a lifestyle — JPR Williams made his most memorable strides on the verdant fields of Ridges, molding his fate in the midst of the kinship and rivalry of the game. His excursion from grassroots rugby to the apex of global approval is one set apart by persistent assurance, unrivaled expertise, and a resolute obligation to greatness.

JPR Williams

Inside these pages, the quintessence of JPR Williams unfurls — a player whose coarseness on the field was matched simply by his unfaltering devotion to the game's qualities off the pitch. His particular ability as a fullback, valiant in safeguard, and jolting in assault, carved his name into rugby legends.

However, this book is about more than just accolades and victories; it digs into the substance of the man behind the shirt. Past the stuffed arenas and boisterous cheers, JPR Williams uncovers his excursion past rugby — the difficulties confronted, the illustrations learned, and the permanent imprint left on the game and its local area.

Through meetings, tales, and an excursion through the ups and downs of his life, "In Quest for Rugby Magnificence" lays out an exhaustive representation of a rugby titan whose heritage rises above simple measurements and triumphs, epitomizing the very soul and soul of the game.

JPR Williams

Go along with us on an arresting odyssey through the life, wins, and getting through tradition of JPR Williams — an excursion that typifies the substance of rugby itself.

CHAPTER 1: WHO IS JPR WILLIAMS

A Welsh rugby legend known by his full name of John Peter Rhys Williams, JPR Williams is associated with skill, bravery, and dedication in the sport. Brought into the world on Walk 2, 1949, in Bridgend, Ribs, Williams experienced childhood in a climate saturated with rugby custom. He would later turn into a notorious figure in the realm of rugby, especially prestigious for his exhibitions as a fullback.

Standing apart for his uncommon physicality, adaptability, and unflinching responsibility on the field, JPR Williams leaving a permanent imprint on the game during the 1960s and 1970s. He acquired inescapable acknowledgment for his residency with the Welsh public group, accomplishing various awards all through his famous lifetime. Williams made his worldwide

JPR Williams

presentation for Ridges in 1969 and proceeded to get an extraordinary standing as a critical figure in the group's victories.

One of his central traits was his brave way to deal with the game, apparent in his extraordinary cautious capacities and his surprising skill to counterattack from the back. Prestigious for his 'straightforward' way to deal with rugby, he was a scary power on the pitch, succeeding in his job as a fullback because of his faultless handling, positional sense, and hostile abilities.

Williams' commitment reached out past public limits as he was likewise an imperative individual from the English and Irish Lions. He partook in visits with the Lions, eminently in New Zealand in 1971, where his exhibitions hardened his place as one of the game's most regarded and respected players. His steady devotion and remarkable exhibitions in these visits additionally established his status as a rugby legend.

JPR Williams

Off the field, JPR Williams sought after a lifelong in medication, exhibiting a different arrangement of gifts past his rugby ability. He adjusted his life as an expert rugby player with an effective profession as a specialist, showing the two his scholarly keenness and his capacity to succeed in various circles.

JPR Williams is still a significant figure in rugby despite his retirement from the sport. His inheritance gets through for his on-field heroics as well as for the qualities he epitomized — respectability, versatility, and a profound energy for the game. His effect on rugby culture, both in Grains and globally, keeps on moving ages of hopeful rugby players and fans, leaving a remarkable heritage inside the game.

1.1 EARLY DAYS

JPR Williams

John Peter Rhys Williams, all the more generally known as JPR Williams, was brought into the world on Walk 2, 1949, in Bridgend, Grains, making way for a daily existence profoundly settled in the rich rugby legacy of his country. Experiencing childhood in Ridges during the mid-twentieth 100 years, rugby was something other than a game — it was a social establishment and a lifestyle. Since the beginning, Williams was drenched in this climate, where rugby was commended and venerated, establishing the groundwork for his future in the game.

As a kid, Williams showed promising athletic capacities and a characteristic tendency towards rugby. He improved his abilities playing rugby in the schoolyards and neighborhood clubs, where his enthusiasm for the game started to thrive. His early stages were set apart by an unflinching devotion to the game, going through innumerable hours working on, fostering his procedure, and leveling up his skills on the field.

JPR Williams

Williams' initial rugby venture was formed by the upsides of difficult work, fellowship, and devotion imparted in him by guides, mentors, and the rugby local area. His ability immediately became clear, acquiring him acknowledgment and deference among his companions and mentors.

It was during his early stages, through school rugby and neighborhood club contests, that JPR Williams laid the foundation for what might later turn into a momentous profession. His initial days in the game were portrayed by a profound love for the game, a yearn for development, and a developing standing as a tremendous ability — an establishment whereupon he would fabricate his inheritance as quite possibly of rugby's most notable figure.

The establishments laid during his experience growing up and juvenile years in Ridges would demonstrate critical in molding Williams' direction in rugby, making way for a vocation characterized by expertise, assurance, and a tenacious quest for greatness on the rugby field.

JPR Williams

1.2 CHILDHOOD INFLUENCES

JPR Williams' life as a youngster was profoundly impacted by the rich embroidery of Welsh culture, where rugby held an exceptional spot in the hearts of many. Experiencing childhood in Bridgend, a town with a solid rugby custom, Williams was encircled by a local area that inhaled, lived, and commended the game. The air was pervaded with rugby enthusiasm, and this unavoidable energy for the game turned into a basic piece of his childhood.

Rugby was more than just a sport in his family; it was a tradition that was passed down through the generations. Williams was presented to the game since the beginning, with relatives sharing accounts of rugby legends, matches, and the pride related with addressing Ridges on the worldwide stage. These familial impacts imparted in him a profound appreciation for the game's legacy and values.

Besides, the nearby local area assumed a huge part in forming Williams' rugby process. Bridgend, known for its rugby enthusiasm, gave a climate where rugby was not only a game played on ends of the week; it was a point of convergence of local area life. The fellowship, backing, and energy of the local area for the game encouraged a feeling of having a place and enthusiasm inside Williams, impacting his devotion to rugby.

Also, the good examples and rugby symbols of the time filled in as motivations for youthful Williams. Welsh rugby legends, whose names reverberated through the roads and arenas, became icons for him. With their feats and accomplishments, these figures served as beacons of aspiration, influencing his aspirations and shaping his dreams of one day sporting the Wales' iconic red jersey.

The mix of familial impact, local area soul, and deference for rugby legends generally added to the

JPR Williams

development of JPR Williams' well established association with the game. These youth impacts touched off his energy for rugby as well as imparted in him the upsides of cooperation, commitment, and sportsmanship that would portray his renowned lifetime and leave a persevering through influence on the universe of rugby.

1.3 SPORTING BEGINNINGS

JPR Williams' brandishing starting points were set apart by an intense energy for rugby that immediately turned into a characterizing part of his life. From his initial a very long time in Bridgend, Ridges, Williams showed a natural ability and love for the game, making way for a wonderful excursion in the realm of rugby.

His underlying introductions to coordinated rugby happened during his school days, where he exhibited his athletic ability on the rugby fields. His talent began to

JPR Williams

shine here, drawing the attention of both his peers and coaches. Williams put in a lot of time training, improving his skills, and learning about the game, demonstrating his dedication to the sport.

His inherent capacities and obligation to rugby drove him to nearby clubs, where he proceeded to thrive and sharpen his art. The club climate gave a road to Williams to additional sustain his ability while submerging himself in the cutthroat idea of the game. His exhibitions at the club level set his standing as a promising youthful player inside the Welsh rugby local area.

As he advanced through the positions, Williams' devotion to rugby strengthened. In addition to his playing prowess, he displayed leadership qualities that distinguished him. His assurance, hard working attitude, and a profound comprehension of the game before long gathered consideration past the nearby club scene.

Williams' donning starting points were described by a determined quest for greatness. His movement from

JPR Williams

school rugby to club contests established the groundwork for his future achievement. These early encounters in the game exhibited his innate capacities as well as imparted in him the upsides of collaboration, discipline, and flexibility — credits that would become signs of his famous rugby vocation.

1.4 PASSION FOR RUGBY AWAKENS

During his formative years, JPR Williams' passion for rugby grew into an unwavering dedication that would set the course of his life. Experiencing childhood in a rugby-driven climate in Bridgend, Ribs, Williams was drenched in a culture that loved the game. His openness to rugby since the beginning lighted a flash inside him, igniting a significant love and interest for the game.

The adventure of watching neighborhood matches, hearing stories of rugby legends, and seeing the enthusiasm of the local area during rugby occasions profoundly affected Williams. He was deeply moved by the emotional connection that was made between the sport and Welsh culture, which laid the groundwork for his lifelong commitment to rugby.

As he started effectively partaking in rugby during his school days, Williams found a feeling of direction and euphoria on the rugby field. The adrenaline surge of contending, the kinship among partners, and the excitement of planning and executing plays energized his energy further. Rugby turned out to be something other than a game — it turned into a fundamental piece of his character.

Williams' enthusiasm for rugby wasn't exclusively about the adventure of rivalry; it incorporated a significant appreciation for the qualities inserted inside the game. He embraced the ethos of collaboration, discipline, and sportsmanship, understanding that rugby was about individual ability as well as about aggregate exertion and solidarity.

JPR Williams

The more profoundly elaborate Williams became in rugby, the more his energy developed. His tenacious quest for development, his want achievement, and his affection for the game kept on escalating. A remarkable rugby career that was marked by dedication, skill, and an unwavering commitment to the sport he cherished was paved over by this growing passion. Eventually, his enthusiasm for rugby characterized his excursion in the game as well as left a getting through heritage inside the records of Welsh and worldwide rugby history.

JPR Williams

CHAPTER 2: RISE TO PROMINENCE

In the narratives of JPR Williams' profession, the section named "Ascend to Conspicuousness" denotes a significant stage in his excursion inside the rugby clique. This chapter delves into his rise from the grassroots level to national and international recognition as a formidable force in rugby.

Williams' rise to fame began during his school rugby days, when people started to notice his extraordinary abilities. His exhibitions on the field were imperative, displaying his inherent capacities and faithful commitment to the game. This period established the groundwork for his future triumphs, as mentors and eyewitnesses perceived his true capacity as a champion player.

Moving past school rugby, Williams changed to club rugby, where his gifts kept on prospering. His obligation

JPR Williams

to preparing, combined with his natural abilities, put him aside from his friends. He succeeded in club contests, further establishing his standing as a rising star inside the Welsh rugby scene.

His leap forward onto the public stage was an extremely important occasion in his excursion. Williams procured his most memorable cap for Grains in 1969, denoting the beginning of a heavenly global vocation. His exhibitions on the global stage were downright phenomenal, procuring him far reaching recognition and laying out him as a key part of the Welsh public group.

During this period, Williams' ascent to noticeable quality was described by his reliable greatness on the field. His commitments to Ridges' achievements in different competitions and matches turned into the stuff of legend. His talented play as a fullback, set apart by strong safeguard, exceptional spryness, and a capacity to counterattack successfully, collected deference from fans and rivals alike.

In addition, not only did his performance in crucial tournaments and matches earn him praise, but they also significantly contributed to the team's success. Williams arose as a pioneer, through his on-field ability as well as through his assurance and obligation to the Welsh reason.

This part typifies a significant stage in Williams' profession — a time of quick climb from a promising ability to a rugby symbol. His rise to prominence was not solely due to his own success; It was evidence of his tenacity, commitment, and unwavering enthusiasm for the game. The path he took during this stage of his career laid the groundwork for the legendary status he would eventually achieve in rugby history.

2.1 SCHOOL RUGBY DAYS

JPR Williams' school rugby days address a fundamental period that laid the basis for his renowned lifetime in the

JPR Williams

game. Experiencing childhood in Bridgend, Ribs, Williams was acquainted with rugby at an early age, and his school years turned into the material whereupon his ability and enthusiasm for the game were sharpened and exhibited.

Williams showed a natural aptitude for rugby while he was in school, which quickly drew coaches and other students' attention. He had a natural physicality and a profound comprehension of the game, which put him aside as a champion player. His exhibitions on the school rugby fields were set apart by ability, assurance, and a resolute obligation to greatness.

As a youthful player, Williams drenched himself in the way of life of school rugby, embracing the kinship among colleagues and the excitement of cutthroat matches. These early stages gave a climate where he fostered his specialized capacities as well as soaked up the qualities basic to rugby - discipline, collaboration, and strength.

JPR Williams

Williams' school rugby days filled in as a pivotal formative stage, giving him the stage to exhibit his ability and commitment. His excellent exhibitions during this period acquired him acknowledgment inside the school as well as laid the foundation for his movement to more significant levels of rivalry.

In addition, his school rugby experiences cultivated his competitive spirit and fueled his enthusiasm for the sport. It was during these early stages that Williams produced a profound close to home association with rugby, molding his goals and making way for a future set apart by surprising accomplishments on the rugby field.

The examples learned and the encounters acquired during his school rugby days turned into a vital piece of Williams' excursion, molding his personality and imparting in him the qualities that would characterize his distinguished lifetime. These early years were a demonstration of his devotion, ability, and the establishment whereupon he would fabricate an

JPR Williams

inheritance as quite possibly of rugby's most notorious figure.

2.2 CLUB BEGINNINGS

The transition that JPR Williams made from school rugby to club rugby was a significant step on his path to becoming a well-known rugby player. Joining neighborhood clubs after his school days, Williams ended up in the midst of a more serious and moving climate that permitted him to additionally refine his abilities and exhibit his expanding ability on a more extensive stage.

As he wandered into club rugby, Williams immediately had an effect, standing apart among his friends with his outstanding physicality and rugby ability. He quickly became a part of the club's culture and immersed himself in a setting that valued teamwork, dedication, and excellence. His obligation to the game and his constant hard working attitude immediately became clear to colleagues and mentors.

Playing for nearby clubs furnished Williams with a more organized and serious stage to hoist his game. The more elevated level of rivalry and the chance to confront rivals from various foundations and ranges of abilities permitted him to grow his rugby collection and develop as a player.

Besides, club rugby gave Williams the opportunity to gain from experienced players, mentors, and coaches inside the rugby local area. Their direction and backing assumed a urgent part in molding his improvement as a player and imparting in him the strategic subtleties and better parts of the game.

In Welsh rugby circles, his performances in club competitions established his reputation as a rising star. Williams' commitments to his club's victories and his predictable presentations of ability and assurance further reinforced his remaining inside the rugby clique.

Past individual achievements, his time in club rugby supported his feeling of fellowship and cooperation — values that would stay fundamental to his playing style and ethos all through his profession. The club climate filled in as a pot where his ability was refined, his commitment tried, and his energy for the game extended.

At last, Williams' club starting points laid the foundation for the accomplishments that would follow. His rugby journey was greatly influenced by the experiences, lessons, and relationships he developed during this phase of his career. They also shaped the course of his illustrious rugby career.

2.3 NATIONAL RECOGNITION

JPR Williams

JPR Williams' climb to public acknowledgment remains as a characterizing section in his celebrated rugby vocation. Subsequent to improving his abilities in school and club rugby, Williams procured the honor of addressing Ridges on the worldwide stage — a summit of his devotion, ability, and immovable obligation to the game.

Williams made his global presentation for Ridges in 1969, a groundbreaking event that obvious the conventional affirmation of his ability as a rugby player. Venturing onto the field decorated in the notorious red shirt, he set out on an excursion that would draw his name into the records of Welsh rugby history. His determination for the public group was a demonstration of the outstanding abilities he had displayed during his early stages.

As a fullback, Williams immediately turned into a key part in the Welsh setup. His exhibitions on the global stage were described by a bold way to deal with the game, strong guarded capacities, and a capacity to

JPR Williams

contribute essentially in both assault and safeguard. These characteristics charmed him to fans and acquired him the profound respect of colleagues and adversaries the same.

Public acknowledgment was not exclusively about individual accomplishment for Williams; It was about showing pride in his country and embodying the Welsh rugby spirit. His exhibitions in key matches and competitions, like the Five Countries Title, became extremely important occasions in his vocation, lifting him to the situation with a rugby symbol.

Williams' effect stretched out past the pitch, as he turned into an image of Welsh rugby greatness. His commitments to Grains' triumphs, including Huge homerun triumphs, further cemented his place among the rugby first class. His standing as a determined, trustworthy player and a pioneer inside the group developed with every worldwide appearance.

JPR Williams

Being perceived as a vital participant for Ridges likewise carried with it the heaviness of assumptions. Williams bore this obligation with beauty, reliably conveying champion exhibitions that charmed him to the Welsh rugby devoted. His obligation to the public reason turned into a wellspring of motivation for hopeful players and an important matter for the whole country.

In the more extensive rugby local area, JPR Williams' public acknowledgment raised him to a status where his name became inseparable from greatness. His excursion from nearby clubs to the global field exemplified the zenith of accomplishment in Welsh rugby, and his heritage as a public symbol perseveres as a demonstration of his effect on the game.

JPR Williams

CHAPTER 3: THE RED JERSEY

In JPR Williams' story, the chapter titled "The Red Jersey" is a crucial section that describes his experience wearing the famous Welsh rugby jersey. Addressing Ribs, represented by the venerated red pullover, was both an honor and an obligation that characterized Williams' vocation and inheritance inside the rugby domain.

Williams' enlistment into the Welsh public group denoted the start of a section where his exhibitions on the global stage would turn into the stuff of legend. The red pullover, saturated with history and custom, connoted a uniform as well as a significant association with Welsh personality and the enthusiasm of a country for the game.

As a fullback, Williams brought a special and impressive range of abilities to the group. His courageous way to deal with the game, vigorous protective capacities, and

JPR Williams

an uncanny capacity to add to both going after and guarded periods of play made him a key part in the Welsh setup. Williams painted his legacy on the red jersey, which he wore with pride, match after match.

The imagery of the red shirt reached out past individual exhibitions. Williams turned into an image of Welsh rugby greatness, epitomizing the strength, diligence, and expertise that the country held dear. His commitments to noteworthy triumphs and Huge homerun wins raised him to a worshipped status, getting his place among the pantheon of Welsh rugby greats.

The part unfurls with records of vital minutes in the red pullover - the adrenaline-siphoning public hymns, the energizing thunder of the group, and the furious fights on the rugby field. Williams' dedication to the team and his capacity to deliver under pressure established him as a symbol of Welsh rugby spirit and inscribed his name in the hearts of fans.

JPR Williams

Besides, the red pullover addressed a fellowship and brotherhood produced with partners. Every match became a collective effort to honor the jersey's legacy and the nation it represented due to the players' shared pride in wearing the Welsh colors.

"The Red Jersey" fills in as a demonstration of Williams' getting through heritage in Welsh rugby. His journey in that iconic uniform exemplifies not only his individual brilliance but also the collective spirit and fervor of international rugby. This part remains as a recognition for Williams' commitments to Welsh rugby history and the permanent imprint he left on the game while wearing the worshipped red shirt.

3.1 WALES DEBUT

JPR Williams' presentation for Grains remains as a milestone second in his celebrated rugby profession,

JPR Williams

denoting the commencement of an excursion that would reclassify the scene of Welsh rugby. The summit of long stretches of devotion and difficult work, his presentation was a demonstration of his outstanding ability and the acknowledgment of his commitments to the game.

Williams made his debut for Wales against England in the Five Nations Championship on January 18, 1969. The meaning of this second was not lost on him, as he ventured onto the consecrated rugby grounds enhanced in the famous red shirt — an image of public pride and a demonstration of his climb to the most elevated echelons of the game.

As a somewhat youthful player at that point, Williams' choice for the public group was a demonstration of his remarkable exhibitions in school and club rugby. The presentation addressed an individual accomplishment as well as an approval of his obligation to the game and an acknowledgment of his capability to have a massive effect on the worldwide stage.

JPR Williams

The match against Britain turned into a pot where Williams exhibited his abilities and declared his appearance as an amazing powerhouse in Welsh rugby. His intrepid playstyle, set apart by strong protection and a readiness to add to going after plays, immediately charmed him to fans and gained him appreciation among colleagues and rivals alike.

Past the singular honors, Williams' introduction for Ribs denoted the start of a time of huge accomplishment for the public group. His consideration in the setup added a unique component to the crew, and his exhibitions assumed a pivotal part in Grains' triumphs in ensuing matches.

The introduction additionally set the vibe for Williams' getting through relationship with the Welsh pullover. Wearing the red pullover turned into a wellspring of gigantic pride for him, representing individual accomplishment as well as the aggregate yearnings of a country energetic about rugby.

JPR Williams

By and large, JPR Williams' Ridges debut fills in as a crucial section in the more extensive story of Welsh rugby. It denoted the development of a rugby symbol who might proceed to make a permanent imprint on the game, addressing the embodiment of expertise, devotion, and public pride each time he took the field in the red shirt.

3.2 INTERNATIONAL TRIUMPHS

JPR Williams' global victories comprise a superb section in the story of Welsh rugby, a story written in triumphs, versatility, and notable minutes on the stupendous stage. From his presentation in 1969, Williams left on an excursion that would see him contribute fundamentally to Ribs' progress in different worldwide rivalries, making a permanent imprint on the game.

JPR Williams

One of the zenith minutes came in 1971 during the English and Irish Lions' visit to New Zealand. Williams assumed a urgent part in this memorable series, exhibiting his brand name daring style and protective dominance. His exhibitions, especially in the third test, added to the Lions' most memorable series triumph against the All Blacks in New Zealand — a fantastic accomplishment that cemented Williams' status as a rugby legend.

On the Five Countries stage, Williams assumed an instrumental part in Ribs' strength during the mid 1970s. His appearances were inseparable from furious contest, vital brightness, and unflinching responsibility. Williams added to Grains getting Huge homerun triumphs in 1971, 1976, and 1978, setting up a good foundation for himself as a key part in a group that reliably arrived at the zenith of European rugby.

Besides, Williams' strength and effect were apparent in his job during Grains' Triple Crown wins. His capacity to lift his game in essential minutes, combined with his

38

JPR Williams

initiative on the field, had a vital impact in Ridges' prosperity against their Home Countries rivals. Each win added to Williams' own honors as well as enhanced the rugby tradition of Ribs during that period.

The summit of his worldwide victories was maybe best exemplified in the 1976 Five Countries Title, where Ridges accomplished a Huge homerun under Williams' captaincy. His initiative characteristics came to the front, directing an imposing Welsh group through a moving competition to get a decisive victory of triumphs — a demonstration of his impact both as a player and a commander.

Past the measurements and prizes, Williams' global victories exemplify the soul of Welsh rugby during a brilliant time. His responsibility, determination, and dominance of the game added to a time of supported achievement that left a persevering through influence on the game. JPR Williams stays a venerated figure for the triumphs he got as well as for how he played the game

JPR Williams

— a valiant, persistent quest for win that reverberates in the chronicles of worldwide rugby history.

3.3 LION TOUR SUCCESS

JPR Williams' prosperity during the English and Irish Lions' visit to New Zealand in 1971 stands as a famous section in the two his vocation and the records of rugby history. This visit is much of the time viewed as quite possibly of the main accomplishment in Lions history, and Williams assumed a significant part in the group's victory against the powerful All Blacks.

As the Lions' fullback, Williams exhibited his bold and solid style of play, procuring him the epithet "The Iron Duke." His strong cautious abilities, exemplified by his bold handling, turned into a key part for the Lions all through the visit. His efforts not only prevented the formidable New Zealand attackers from scoring, but they also inspired his teammates.

The series against the All Blacks was firmly challenged, with Williams' commitment turning out to be progressively essential. In the third and last test, Williams' take a stab at saving tackle on Fergie McCormick became meaningful of his obligation to the Lions' goal. The Lions got a notable 14-14 draw, securing the series 2-1 and denoting the primary series triumph against New Zealand starting around 1959.

Williams' impact reached out past his playing skills; his authority characteristics were apparent all through the visit. While not the authority commander, he expected a true influential position, gaining the appreciation and deference of his partners. His quiet disposition under tension and his capacity to rouse and join the crew were instrumental in the Lions' progress in New Zealand.

The visit's prosperity launch Williams into rugby fables, laying out him as a legend in Ridges as well as across the

JPR Williams

English Isles. His exhibitions against New Zealand displayed the industriousness and expertise that characterized his vocation, making him an image of Lions' versatility and assurance.

The meaning of the 1971 Lions visit goes past the triumphs on the field. It denoted a turning point in rugby history, testing the view of power encompassing New Zealand rugby. JPR Williams, with his unstoppable soul and unflinching responsibility, assumed a basic part in this extraordinary section, procuring his place among the pantheon of rugby greats.

JPR Williams

CHAPTER 4: THE ART OF FULLBACK PLAY

The part named "The Craft of Fullback Play" dives into JPR Williams' dominance of the fullback position, unwinding the complexities that made him an unmatched power on the rugby field. As a fullback, Williams re-imagined the assumptions for the position, consolidating protective strength, strategic knowledge, and hostile energy in a way that made a permanent imprint on the game.

Williams' style was characterized by his defensive prowess. He became a formidable obstacle for opposing attackers because of his fearless tackling and last-ditch interventions. His capacity to peruse the game, expect the developments of rivals, and execute exact handles set his standing as quite possibly of the best cautious fullback in rugby history. Williams' cautious abilities

JPR Williams

ruined endless resistance assaults as well as imparted a feeling of trust in his colleagues.

Williams, however, was more than just a reliable defensive player; he carried a creative and going after aspect to the fullback position. His counterattacking skills were extraordinary, frequently transforming guarded circumstances into chances to take advantage of resistance shortcomings. Whether through jolting runs or very much planned passes, Williams had a talent for infusing speed and unconventionality into the game. He became a dual threat as a result of his offensive contributions, which allowed him to have an impact on both the offensive and defensive sides of a game.

Strategically, Williams was a visionary fullback. His positional mindfulness and comprehension of the game's subtleties permitted him to direct play from the back. Whether marshaling the cautious line, giving an extra playmaking choice, or executing key kicks, Williams' dynamic on the field displayed a profound comprehension of the game's intricacies. His capacity to

JPR Williams

control the rhythm and heading of play made him a player as well as a strategist on the pitch.

Williams' dedication to training and persistent pursuit of improvement demonstrated his dedication to perfecting the art of fullback play off the field. His hard working attitude and steady quest for greatness set a norm for hopeful fullbacks and added to the development of the position.

"The Craft of Fullback Play" gives recognition to JPR Williams' complex commitments as a fullback. It disentangles the layers of his protective dominance, going after splendor, and strategic sharpness, arranging a thorough representation of a player whose impact rose above the conventional limits of his situation, leaving a getting through heritage in the pantheon of rugby's extraordinary fullbacks.

JPR Williams

4.1 DEFENSIVE MASTERY

In the long and illustrious history of rugby, JPR Williams's defensive mastery defines his identity as a fullback. Prestigious for his dauntless and unflinching handling, Williams raised protective play to an artistic expression, setting an unrivaled norm for the people who might emulate his example.

At the core of Williams' guarded ability was his remarkable capacity to peruse the game. His sharp comprehension of rivals' developments, key expectation, and an intuitive handle of the back and forth movement of a match permitted him to situate himself capably on the field. This natural feeling of where he should have been empowered Williams to execute exact handles, reliably impeding resistance assaults and showing an unmatched authority of guarded situating.

JPR Williams

What put Williams aside was his procedure as well as the sheer fortitude he brought to the guarded part of the game. His handles were described by a resolute responsibility, frequently making him the last line of safeguard with match-saving mediations. Williams' mental fortitude in the tackle enlivened his colleagues as well as imparted a feeling of dread in restricting aggressors who realized they were facing a guarded maestro.

Besides, Williams' genuineness and hostility in protection were supplemented by a natural capacity to upset resistance plays. His timing and execution of tackles frequently transformed cautious circumstances into open doors for counterattacks. Williams changed guard into a proactive component of his game, a demonstration of his essential comprehension of how protective greatness could be an impetus for hostile energy.

His defensive contributions became a defining feature of his international career beyond individual matches.

JPR Williams

Williams made light of a urgent job in closing probably the most imposing assailants in the rugby world during his period, making him a priceless resource for the two Ridges and the English and Irish Lions.

In outline, JPR Williams' protective dominance wasn't just about halting adversaries; it was tied in with reshaping the job of a fullback into a protective key part. His ability to read the game, make precise tackles, and lead by example with unmatched courage left an indelible mark, inspiring subsequent generations of fullbacks to strive for defensive excellence on the rugby field similar to his.

4.2 ATTACKING PROWESS

JPR Williams' going after ability as a fullback was a characterizing component of his play, adding a dynamic and unusual aspect to his job on the rugby field. While prestigious for his cautious dominance, Williams

JPR Williams

exhibited a similarly strong capacity to contribute unpleasantly, making him perhaps of the most ridiculously complete and significant player throughout the entire existence of the game.

One of the signs of Williams' going after game was his extraordinary abilities to counterattack. Situated somewhere down in the backfield, he had a natural feeling of when to infuse pace into the game, transforming cautious circumstances into potential chances to take advantage of resistance shortcomings. Williams was able to maneuver through opposing defenses with remarkable ease because of his acceleration, agility, and vision. He frequently left defenders in his wake as he launched counterattacks that enthralled crowds and demoralized opponents.

In addition, Williams was an effective ball-handler as well as a skilled runner. His capacity to time and execute very much positioned passes, frequently including many-sided transaction with partners, exhibited a degree of playmaking seldom seen from a fullback. This

JPR Williams

playmaking aspect added an additional layer of capriciousness to his assaults, as he consistently changed from a protective job to an essential giver in the group's hostile methodologies.

Williams' contribution in going after set pieces, especially during line tears and open-field play, further featured his adaptability. Whether starting have a go at scoring valuable open doors or polishing off moves himself, he turned into a fundamental connection between the forward pack and the backs, showing a nuanced comprehension of the game that reached out past cautious obligations.

Significantly, Williams' going after ability wasn't bound to individual brightness; it supplemented the aggregate methodologies of the groups he addressed. His hostile commitments became basic to the general progress of Ridges and the English and Irish Lions during his profession. Williams' impact in attacking situations frequently shifted the momentum, eliciting brilliant

JPR Williams

moments that etched his name into the memories of rugby fans all over the world.

In synopsis, JPR Williams' going after ability was a demonstration of his flexibility and his capacity to impact the game at the two closures of the field. He set the standard for fullbacks with his brilliant counterattacking, playmaking, and strategic involvement in attacking plays. He also influenced the development of the position and left an indelible mark on the art of attacking play in rugby history.

4.3 TACTICAL BRILLIANCE

JPR Williams' strategic splendor as a fullback put him aside as a genius on the rugby field, rising above the conventional jobs related with his situation. His clever comprehension of the game's intricacies, combined with key intuition, permitted him to direct play, marshal

JPR Williams

protective lines, and contribute definitively to his group's general strategies.

A vital component of Williams' strategic brightness was his extraordinary positional mindfulness. He was always in the right place at the right time, whether he was stationed deep to field kicks or strategically placed in open play. This natural feeling of situating not just permitted him to be a powerful last line of guard yet additionally situated him as a playmaker fit for starting assaults or giving a significant connection in the hostile chain.

Williams' dynamic on the field was set apart by a mix of insight and logic. As a fullback, he had the obligation of evaluating the unfurling elements of the match, making split-second decisions on whether to kick, pass, or run. He set an example for other players in his position by being able to make sound decisions under pressure.

Notwithstanding his job as a protective sturdy and going after impetus, Williams was a strategist in the kicking

JPR Williams

game. His exact and key kicks assuage pressure, acquired regional benefit, and upset resistance methodologies. Whether executing all around put kicks for contact or conveying pinpoint kicks into open spaces, Williams' kicking abilities turned into a vital piece of his strategic collection, adding to his group's general blueprint.

Administration assumed a vital part in Williams' strategic impact on the field. Indeed, even without holding an authority captaincy job in each match, his on-field administration was apparent in directing protective designs, arranging plays, and rousing colleagues. Williams' administration as a visual demonstration and his capacity to impart successfully on the pitch added to the general union and execution of well defined courses of action.

Williams' strategic brightness was not restricted to one aspect of the game; It included a comprehensive comprehension of the complexities of rugby. His capacity to consistently change between protective,

JPR Williams

going after, and key jobs made him a complex player, and his effect on the strategic components of matches highlighted his importance as a rugby visionary.

In synopsis, JPR Williams' strategic splendor was the consequence of an extensive range of abilities, key foreknowledge, and a profound comprehension of the subtleties of rugby. His impact on the field went past individual plays, leaving a getting through heritage that reshaped view of the fullback position and exhibited the imaginativeness of strategic play in the game.

JPR Williams

CHAPTER 5: BEYOND THE PITCH

JPR Williams' strategic splendor as a fullback put him aside as a genius on the rugby field, rising above the conventional jobs related with his situation. His clever comprehension of the game's intricacies, combined with key intuition, permitted him to direct play, marshal protective lines, and contribute definitively to his group's general strategies.

A vital component of Williams' strategic brightness was his extraordinary positional mindfulness. He was always in the right place at the right time, whether he was stationed deep to field kicks or strategically placed in open play. This natural feeling of situating not just permitted him to be a powerful last line of guard yet additionally situated him as a playmaker fit for starting assaults or giving a significant connection in the hostile chain.

JPR Williams

Williams' dynamic on the field was set apart by a mix of insight and logic. As a fullback, he had the obligation of evaluating the unfurling elements of the match, making split-second decisions on whether to kick, pass, or run. He set an example for other players in his position by being able to make sound decisions under pressure.

Notwithstanding his job as a protective sturdy and going after impetus, Williams was a strategist in the kicking game. His exact and key kicks assuage pressure, acquired regional benefit, and upset resistance methodologies. Whether executing all around put kicks for contact or conveying pinpoint kicks into open spaces, Williams' kicking abilities turned into a vital piece of his strategic collection, adding to his group's general blueprint.

Administration assumed a vital part in Williams' strategic impact on the field. Indeed, even without holding an authority captaincy job in each match, his on-field administration was apparent in directing protective designs, arranging plays, and rousing colleagues. Williams' administration as a visual demonstration and his capacity to impart successfully on the pitch added to the general union and execution of well defined courses of action.

Williams' strategic brightness was not restricted to one aspect of the game; It included a comprehensive comprehension of the complexities of rugby. His capacity to consistently change between protective, going after, and key jobs made him a complex player, and his effect on the strategic components of matches highlighted his importance as a rugby visionary.

In synopsis, JPR Williams' strategic splendor was the consequence of an extensive range of abilities, key foreknowledge, and a profound comprehension of the subtleties of rugby. His impact on the field went past individual plays, leaving a getting through heritage that reshaped view of the fullback position and exhibited the imaginativeness of strategic play in the game.

JPR Williams

5.1 LIFE BEYOND RUGBY

JPR Williams' life past rugby is a demonstration of the profundity and variety of his personality, displaying a man whose effect stretched out a long ways past the limits of the rugby pitch. His successful medical career was one of the most memorable aspects of his life after rugby. Williams, notwithstanding the thorough requests of his rugby profession, sought after a physician certification and proceeded to turn into a cultivated muscular specialist. This double achievement featured his scholarly ability as well as exemplified his obligation to contributing genuinely to society outside the domain of sports.

As a clinical expert, Williams zeroed in on sports-related wounds, utilizing his cozy information on the actual requests of rugby to give particular consideration to competitors. His skill in muscular health and sports medication made him a regarded figure in the clinical

58

local area, displaying an ability to succeed in the field of rugby as well as in the perplexing and requesting field of medical services.

Socially, JPR Williams turned into a getting through image of Welsh character. His exhibitions on the rugby field, set apart by flexibility, assurance, and a savage feeling of public pride, resounded profoundly with the Welsh public. Past the honors and triumphs, Williams turned into a social symbol, encapsulating the soul of Welsh rugby greatness and remaining as a wellspring of motivation for ages of rugby devotees in Ridges.

Williams' impact stretched out to the more extensive rugby local area, where he assumed a critical part in the turn of events and advancement of the game. Whether through tutoring youthful players, training, or supporting for the proceeded with development of rugby at different levels, Williams remained profoundly engaged with the game that had characterized a critical piece of his life. His obligation to rugby's improvement exhibited a

JPR Williams

craving to reward the game and guarantee its persevering through heritage.

Notwithstanding his commitments in medication and rugby, Williams participated in charity and local area administration, highlighting a promise to having a constructive outcome past private accomplishments. His contribution in magnanimous exercises mirrored a more extensive ethos of empathy and a craving to utilize his leverage to improve society. Williams' magnanimous endeavors reflected the upsides of sportsmanship and kinship that he exemplified all through his rugby profession.

In synopsis, JPR Williams' life past rugby embodies an all encompassing and effective presence. His accomplishments in medication, social importance, commitments to rugby, and generosity on the whole paint a representation of a man whose impact reached out a long ways past the attempt lines. Williams' heritage isn't restricted to his ability as a rugby legend however envelops a day to day existence wealthy in achievements, administration, and a guarantee to greatness in different circles.

5.2 PROFESSIONAL CAREER

JPR Williams' expert vocation unfurled as a striking excursion that joined his ability in rugby with an effective and significant endeavor into the field of medication. Following his initial rugby wins, Williams sought after a physician certification, displaying a guarantee to scholarly greatness close by his thriving rugby vocation. This double pursuit featured his capacity to succeed in two requesting disciplines, making way for a remarkable and recognized proficient excursion.

Williams went on to become an orthopedic surgeon who specialized in sports-related injuries in the medical field. His profound comprehension of the actual requests of rugby, combined with his clinical mastery, situated him

JPR Williams

as a pursued figure in the games medication local area. Williams' commitments to muscular health highlighted his scholarly discernment as well as a devotion to further developing the prosperity of competitors, mixing his enthusiasm for sports with his obligation to medical services.

All the while, Williams' rugby vocation arrived at its zenith during a time when the game was still generally novice. Notwithstanding the shortfall of monetary prizes that advanced proficient competitors appreciate, Williams' commitment to rugby stayed steadfast. His exhibitions for Ribs and the English and Irish Lions became unbelievable, stamping him as one of the most notable players of his age. Williams' commitments on the pitch exhibited his athletic ability as well as his initiative characteristics, contributing essentially to his group's victories.

Williams' influence persisted even as rugby entered the professional era, albeit in different capacities. He wandered into training and coaching jobs, imparting his abundance of involvement to arising gifts. Williams' capacity to consistently explore the changing scene of rugby, from a beginner player to a regarded figure in training, mirrored his versatility and persevering through obligation to the development of the game.

Williams' expert profession, portrayed by a double obligation to medication and rugby, featured his capacity to succeed in different spaces. Beyond his own accomplishments, he had an impact on the development of sports and healthcare as a whole. The juxtaposition of his jobs as a specialist and a rugby symbol embodies a day to day existence that flawlessly mixed proficient greatness, an enthusiasm for sports, and a guarantee to the improvement of the two fields. The professional path that JPR Williams has taken exemplifies an individual's capacity to have a significant impact in a variety of spheres of life.

JPR Williams

5.3 PERSONAL PURSUITS

JPR Williams' special goals mirror a complex life driven by a different scope of interests past the rugby pitch and the clinical field. One prominent feature of his own life is his profound commitment with Welsh culture. Williams, brought up in Grains, turned into an image of Welsh personality, epitomizing the strength, pride, and energy related with the country. His special goal of safeguarding and observing Welsh legacy reached out to his social importance as a notable figure, rising above the domains of game and medication.

Past the organized areas of his expert vocation, Williams participated in different special goals that exhibited his obligation to self-improvement and deep rooted learning. His choice to seek after a practitioner training close by his rugby profession highlighted a devotion to scholarly pursuits. A personal philosophy based on curiosity, self-improvement, and a desire to excel in various fields

JPR Williams

is exemplified by this dedication to continuing education.

Williams' special goals additionally stretched out to the domain of magnanimity and local area administration. He advocated for causes he held dear because he was a well-known figure. Whether supporting beneficent drives or effectively partaking in local area administration, Williams showed a feeling of obligation to contribute emphatically to society. His special goals in such manner featured a more extensive ethos of sympathy, empathy, and a guarantee to having a significant effect past individual accomplishments.

A devoted outdoorsman, Williams communicated his affection for nature through special goals like climbing and investigation. This aspect of his life demonstrated a balance between professional sports' intensity and nature's tranquility. Williams' special goals in outside exercises added to his actual prosperity as well as given an outlet to unwinding and revival in the midst of the requests of his profession.

JPR Williams

In his own life, Williams' interests were not exclusively characterized by accomplishments on the rugby field or in the working room. All things being equal, they mirrored an all encompassing way to deal with living — a guarantee to self-awareness, social safeguarding, local area administration, and an association with nature. JPR Williams' special goals structure an essential piece of his heritage, featuring a daily existence wealthy in encounters and values that reach out past the bounds of any solitary job or achievement.

CHAPTER 6: CHALLENGES AND TRIUMPHS

The section named "Difficulties and Wins" in the existence of JPR Williams unfurls as a story of strength, development, and the route of obstacles both on and off the rugby pitch. The physical toll of the sport was one of Williams' major obstacles. Rugby, particularly during his period, was known for its merciless rawness, and Williams, as a fullback famous for valiant handling, encountered his reasonable portion of wounds. The part digs into how he explored these difficulties, showing a steadiness that became significant of his playing style.

Wounds, however considerable enemies, were met with an unstoppable soul by Williams. The story investigates the physical and mental grit expected to defeat misfortunes, go through restoration, and return to top structure. These difficulties, as opposed to deflecting

JPR Williams

him, filled Williams' assurance, adding to his development as a player who vanquished misfortune as well as an image of flexibility for trying competitors.

Wins in Williams' vocation were joined with the difficulties, making a convincing story of defeating difficulty. The chapter sheds light on significant junctures in his rugby career, such as Williams' pivotal role in securing a series victory against the formidable All Blacks during the historic British and Irish Lions tour of New Zealand in 1971. His accomplishments throughout his career are portrayed not as isolated incidents but rather as the culmination of perseverance, brilliant strategic thinking, and an unwavering dedication to the sport.

Off the pitch, the story dives into the difficulties Williams looked in adjusting a requesting clinical vocation with the afflictions of expert rugby. The double pursuits introduced difficulties in using time effectively, yet Williams explored these intricacies with trademark accuracy. His accomplishments went beyond rugby victories to academic excellence and medical success, demonstrating a remarkable capacity to overcome multiple obstacles.

The part investigates the profound ups and downs of Williams' vocation, from Huge homerun triumphs to the awfulness of wounds and losses. It catches the pith of the man behind the rugby legend — an individual who defied difficulties with a steely determination, gained from misfortunes, and arose victorious despite difficulty. The story of difficulties and wins in Williams' day to day existence turns into an impactful demonstration of the intricacies and wins innate in a vocation that rises above sports, embracing the versatility and determination that characterized JPR Williams' heritage.

6.1 INJURIES

JPR Williams

In the story of JPR Williams' renowned rugby vocation, wounds arise as critical and repeating difficulties that tried his actual versatility and mental guts. As a fullback known for his valiant handling and hard and fast responsibility on the field, Williams much of the time wound up amidst the actual power that portrayed rugby during his period. The section enumerating wounds reveals insight into how these afflictions became basic parts of his excursion, forming his playing style as well as his ability to defeat mishaps.

The cost of wounds on Williams' body is chronicled in the story, displaying the actual requests and forfeits inborn in proficient rugby. From the knocks and injuries to additional serious mishaps, every injury turned into a part in his profession, introducing impediments that he expected to explore to keep adding to his group. The cost of wounds is introduced not as an obstruction but rather as a demonstration of Williams' obligation to the game, where actual penances were an intrinsic piece of the quest for greatness.

JPR Williams

The story proceeds to investigate how Williams faced and dealt with these wounds. Restoration and recuperation, both truly and intellectually, become indispensable parts of the story. The cost for his body requested clinical consideration as well as a profound repository of flexibility. Williams' unwavering determination and passion for the game are shown to be reflected in his capacity to undergo rehabilitation, recover from injuries, and return to the field.

Past the actual perspective, the section digs into the mental effect of wounds. The disappointment, the psychological type of being sidelined, and the strength expected to return more grounded are unpredictably woven into the account. The wounds act as snapshots of self-reflection for Williams, permitting him to take advantage of repositories of mental strength that supplemented his actual capacities.

Wins following times of injury recuperation become the profound pinnacles of the story. Whether it's a rebound match or an essential commitment after recovery, each

JPR Williams

victory over injury is introduced as a demonstration of Williams' personality and resolve. Rather than diminishing his legacy, the injuries serve to define the indomitable spirit that characterized his rugby career.

In rundown, the section on wounds in JPR Williams' account depicts these actual mishaps not as obstacles but rather as cauldrons that manufactured his versatility and exhibited his steadfast obligation to the game. It adds a layer of intricacy to the story, making the victories more piercing and the flexibility more honorable, at last adding to the permanent tradition of one of rugby's actual legends.

6.2 SETBACKS

Difficulties in JPR Williams' story unfurl as critical minutes that tried his purpose, displaying the difficulties and obstacles he confronted both in his rugby vocation and special goals. The section on misfortunes gives a

JPR Williams

sagacious investigation into the different difficulties that briefly become sidetracked, just to see him rise again with faithful assurance.

Rugby, with its innate rawness, conveyed difficulties as wounds, which were maybe the most articulated difficulties Williams experienced. The story dives into examples where wounds constrained him to the sidelines, disturbing his mood and immediately changing the direction of his profession. The difficulties coming about because of wounds became piercing points in the story, uncovering the actual cost of the game as well as Williams' flexibility in beating these misfortunes over and over.

The setbacks didn't just happen on the rugby field; they reached out to the mind boggling balance Williams needed to keep up with between his requesting clinical vocation and his energy for rugby. The story investigates minutes where the double pursuits introduced difficulties, calling for fastidious using time effectively and devotion. These misfortunes feature the intricacies

JPR Williams

of keeping up with greatness in both expert spaces and proposition a brief look into the penances Williams made in exploring his diverse life.

Individual difficulties, whether as losses on the rugby field or difficulties in private life, become vital pieces of the account. The part unfurls these minutes not as disservices to Williams' inheritance but rather as fundamental parts that added to his development. The mishaps filled in as pots, forming his personality and bracing his purpose, giving a more profound comprehension of the man behind the rugby legend.

The story of misfortunes is unpredictably attached to the profound ups and downs of Williams' excursion. Every difficulty, whether physical, expert, or individual, is trailed by a story bend of versatility and win. The mishaps become the impetuses for contemplation, learning, and self-awareness, eventually adding to the all-encompassing subject of win over misfortune that characterizes Williams' inheritance.

JPR Williams

All in all, the section on mishaps in JPR Williams' story is a nuanced investigation of the difficulties he confronted and the misfortunes he experienced. It shows setbacks as chapters in a story about perseverance, determination, and the triumph of the human spirit rather than as obstacles. These misfortunes enhance the account, making the inevitable victories more powerful and exhibiting Williams' capacity to transform difficulties into valuable open doors for development and getting through progress.

6.3 MOMENTS OF TRIUMPH

The story of JPR Williams' life is accentuated by snapshots of win, each addressing a high point in his rugby vocation and individual excursion. The section on snapshots of win exemplifies the thrilling highs that characterized his inheritance, exhibiting his athletic ability as well as his versatility, initiative, and the getting through influence he left on the game.

JPR Williams

One of the fundamental victories in Williams' vocation was without a doubt the English and Irish Lions' visit to New Zealand in 1971. The story digs into the meaning of this visit, where Williams assumed a focal part in getting a noteworthy series triumph against the considerable All Blacks. His contributions, particularly his courageous tackling and leadership on the field, became a symbol of the Lions' victory, which was a turning point in the history of rugby.

The section likewise investigates Williams' job in Ridges' Huge homerun triumphs during the Five Countries Title, especially in 1971, 1976, and 1978. These victories cemented Williams' status as a Welsh rugby symbol and exhibited his consistency in conveying outstanding exhibitions at the most significant level. The story gives bits of knowledge into the elements of these title winning efforts, underscoring Williams' effect as a player as well as an impetus for aggregate achievement.

JPR Williams

Williams' captaincy during the 1976 Five Countries Title adds one more layer to the account of win. Driving Ridges to a Huge homerun triumph that year, he exhibited his on-field ability as well as his initiative characteristics. The strategic acumen, resilience, and motivation he brought to the team make him a revered figure in Welsh rugby history are the subject of this chapter.

The victories stretch out past the rugby pitch, including his fruitful clinical profession and commitments to sports medication. The story shows how Williams was able to achieve excellence in both rugby and medicine by seamlessly balancing his professional pursuits. His double victories in these fields feature a surprising ability to succeed across different spaces.

The close to home reverberation of wins is woven all through the story, giving a nuanced comprehension of the man behind the rugby legend. Moments of triumph become defining chapters that demonstrate Williams' impact on the sport, his nation, and his enduring legacy

JPR Williams

as one of rugby's true greats, whether they are savoring personal milestones or celebrating victories in iconic tournaments.

In conclusion, the chapter in JPR Williams' narrative that discusses his triumphs is a celebration of his accomplishments, both on and off the rugby field. These minutes feature athletic greatness as well as strength, initiative, and a multi-layered heritage that rises above the limits of game, making a permanent imprint on the rich embroidery of rugby history.

6.4 LEGACY IN RUGBY

The legacy that rugby legend JPR Williams leaves behind is a significant chapter in the sport's long and illustrious history. It is marked by his athletic brilliance, unwavering dedication, and enduring influence that extends beyond his playing days. The section on his

JPR Williams

rugby inheritance unfurls as a story of impact, exhibiting the getting through engrave he left on the game and the ages of players who followed.

At the core of Williams' rugby heritage is his dauntless soul on the field. Prestigious for his dauntless handling, vital splendor, and resolute obligation to the group's prosperity, he turned into an image of flexibility and assurance. The story digs into explicit matches, notable handles, and authority minutes that set his status as perhaps of the best player throughout the entire existence of rugby, scratching his name into the chronicles of the game.

Williams' impact stretches out past individual awards to group accomplishments, especially during the English and Irish Lions' visit to New Zealand in 1971. The part investigates how his commitments in that memorable series triumph changed him into a rugby legend, hoisting his own heritage as well as adding to the more extensive story of Lions' victories and the difficult mission against the strong All Blacks.

JPR Williams

The legacy story also sheds light on Williams' role in the 1970s' golden age of Welsh rugby. His vital commitments to various Huge homerun triumphs and Five Countries Titles denoted a time of phenomenal accomplishment for Ridges. The story looks at how, during this golden era, Williams' performances, leadership, and consistent excellence became part of the collective identity of Welsh rugby.

Williams' legacy extends beyond his on-field accomplishments to the development of the fullback position. His multi-layered commitments as a safeguard, assailant, and strategist set new principles for fullbacks. The chapter delves into how his innovative style of play shaped the possibilities and expectations associated with the fullback position for subsequent generations of players.

Off the pitch, Williams' heritage appears in his persevering through influence on the more extensive rugby local area. The story investigates his training jobs,

JPR Williams

mentorship of youthful abilities, and promotion for the development of the game. His commitments to rugby's improvement exhibit a pledge to guaranteeing the game's proceeded with progress and significance for people in the future.

In rundown, JPR Williams' heritage in rugby is a multi-layered story of athletic ability, authority, and an enduring engraving on the game's direction. The section unfurls as a demonstration of his getting through impact, not just inside the setting of his playing days however as a figure whose effect reverberates in the continuous story of rugby, making a permanent imprint on the game he energetically served and formed.

JPR Williams

CHAPTER 7: OFF THE FIELD

The part named "Off the Field" in the story of JPR Williams' life offers a charming investigation into the elements of his character, interests, and commitments past the rugby pitch. This section reveals insight into the diverse idea of Williams, uncovering a man who broadened his impact a long ways past the domains of game and medication.

At the core of "Off the Field" is Williams' social importance and his encapsulation of Welsh personality. The story dives into his job as a social symbol, displaying how his exhibitions on the rugby field, set apart by flexibility, enthusiasm, and a furious feeling of public pride, resounded profoundly with the Welsh public. Williams turned out to be in excess of a rugby player; he turned into an image of Welsh greatness and a wellspring of motivation for ages, raising him to a loved status inside the social story of Grains.

JPR Williams

The section likewise investigates Williams' interests in the field of medication, stressing his achievements as a muscular specialist. It gives experiences into how he flawlessly adjusted the requests of a high-profile rugby vocation with the afflictions of a clinical calling. Williams' outcome in the two fields features his scholarly sharpness as well as his ability to succeed in different and requesting fields.

As an outside devotee, the account unfurls Williams' affection for nature and open air exercises. The intensity of professional rugby and the demands of a medical career were balanced by personal pursuits like hiking and exploration. The part portrays a man who tracked down comfort and restoration in the normal world, uncovering a less popular part of his persona past the rugby field.

Besides, "Off the Field" enlightens Williams' generous undertakings and local area commitment. The story investigates how he used his impact to support worthy missions, mirroring a feeling of obligation and a guarantee to having a beneficial outcome on society. Williams' contribution in local area administration turns into a demonstration of the qualities that directed him past individual accomplishments, adding to the improvement of the more extensive local area.

The part closes by interweaving these different features of Williams' life, exhibiting a man whose impact reaches out a long ways past the attempt lines and working rooms. Whether as a social symbol, an effective specialist, an outside lover, or a humanitarian, "Off the Field" lays out an extensive representation of JPR Williams, uncovering a daily existence wealthy in encounters, values, and commitments that rise above the limits of his wearing and expert undertakings.

7.1 INFLUENCE

JPR Williams

The story of JPR Williams' life is dominated by the central idea of his influence on rugby and beyond. This chapter examines how much Williams changed the sport, his neighborhood, and the cultural landscape as a whole. His impact reaches out a long ways past the rugby pitch, exemplifying a heritage that rises above individual accomplishments.

On the rugby field, Williams' impact is tangible through his progressive way to deal with the fullback position. The account investigates how his dynamic style of play, joining guarded dominance with going after ability, re-imagined the assumptions for fullbacks. His impact on resulting ages of players is clear in the advancement of the position, with many looking to imitate his diverse commitments to the game.

As a pioneer, Williams' impact is featured in his captaincy during the 1976 Five Countries Title. The part investigates how his essential sharpness, versatility, and uplifting initiative directed Ridges to a Huge homerun triumph. Williams' influence as captain extends beyond

JPR Williams

match outcomes. During a golden era, he shaped the ethos of Welsh rugby and left an indelible mark on the sport's collective memory.

Off the field, Williams' social impact as a Welsh symbol is a focal point of the story. The part digs into how his exhibitions became emblematic snapshots of public pride, reverberating profoundly with the Welsh public. Williams' impact as a social figure isn't restricted to his having days however perseveres as influence of Ridges' rugby character, mirroring the upsides of flexibility and enthusiasm that he embodied.

In the clinical field, Williams' impact is apparent in his effective profession as a muscular specialist. The story looks at how his knowledge of injuries caused by sports played a role in athletes' health and the development of sports medicine. His impact stretches out past the working room, forming the convergence of rugby and clinical practices.

JPR Williams

Local area commitment and generosity are extra elements of Williams' impact. The part enlightens how he utilized his height to support worthy missions and contribute emphatically to society. His influence in community service demonstrates his determination to have a significant impact beyond his professional activities.

In rundown, the section on impact illustrates JPR Williams as a figure whose effect resonates across numerous circles. His impact on rugby, initiative, Welsh culture, medication, and local area administration on the whole shape a heritage that stretches out a long ways past individual achievements, making a permanent imprint on the game and the more extensive story of his life.

7.2 LEGACY

JPR Williams

JPR Williams' heritage is a rich embroidery woven with strings of rugby splendor, initiative, social importance, and commitments that stretch out a long ways past the attempt lines. The part on inheritance embodies the getting through influence he has left on the game, his country, and the domains of medication and local area administration.

At the center of Williams' inheritance is his permanent engraving on rugby. The story investigates how his dynamic style of play, courageous handling, and key brightness re-imagined the job of the fullback. His heritage as a player reaches out past measurements, etching his name in the records of rugby history as a the pioneer development of the game, leaving an enduring effect on the manner in which fullbacks approach the game.

Initiative structures an essential part of Williams' inheritance, especially his captaincy during the 1976 Five Countries Title. The story reveals insight into how his rousing initiative directed Ridges to a Huge homerun

JPR Williams

triumph. Williams' heritage as a pioneer is one of flexibility, vital discernment, and an enduring obligation to group achievement, adding to a brilliant period in Welsh rugby that stays carved in the aggregate memory.

Williams' cultural significance is also deciphered in the legacy chapter, which depicts him as an iconic figure in Welsh identity. He became a symbol of Welsh excellence thanks to his passionate rugby performances and strong sense of national pride. Williams' heritage in Welsh culture stretches out past rugby, epitomizing the upsides of versatility and assurance that have become natural for the country's rugby ethos.

In the clinical domain, Williams' heritage as a muscular specialist exhibits his obligation to the prosperity of competitors. The account investigates how his commitments to sports medication formed the convergence of rugby and medical care. His heritage in medication is portrayed by a consistent harmony between an effective clinical profession and a celebrated

JPR Williams

rugby venture, exhibiting an ability to succeed in different and requesting fields.

Philanthropy and community service are two more pillars of Williams' legacy. His efforts to make a difference outside of his work reflect a commitment to giving back as the narrative progresses. Williams' heritage in local area administration is a demonstration of the upsides of sympathy and obligation that characterized his personality past the rugby pitch.

In synopsis, the part on heritage winds around together the multi-layered effect of JPR Williams, depicting him as a rugby legend as well as a pioneer, social symbol, clinical expert, and donor. His legacy is evidence of a life lived with excellence, enthusiasm, and a determination to make lasting contributions that resonate across generations and influence spheres.

JPR Williams

7.3 COMMUNITY ENGAGEMENT

JPR Williams' heritage expands essentially into the domain of local area commitment, displaying his obligation to having a beneficial outcome past the rugby pitch and the clinical field. The part on local area commitment investigates how Williams used his impact and height to contribute definitively to society, turning into a figure profoundly engaged with generosity and drives pointed toward further developing the prosperity of networks.

One aspect of Williams' people group commitment is his support for worthy missions. The account digs into how he utilized his unmistakable quality to advocate different drives, whether supporting medical services programs, instructive undertakings, or other magnanimous tasks. Williams' impact filled in as an impetus for bringing issues to light and assets, adding to the improvement of networks out of luck. This part of his local area

JPR Williams

commitment features a feeling of obligation to involve his foundation for everyone's benefit.

The story likewise unfurls Williams' contribution in local area administration, exhibiting an active way to deal with having a constructive outcome. Whether partaking in local area occasions, coaching trying competitors, or effectively adding to nearby drives, he showed an individual obligation to being straightforwardly engaged with the networks he tried to serve. Williams' people group administration reflects a humanitarian signal as well as a certified association and commitment with individuals he expected to inspire.

As a social symbol in Grains, Williams' people group commitment included a specific reverberation inside the country. The story investigates how his impact stretched out past rugby to epitomize Welsh ethics of flexibility, assurance, and a profound feeling of local area. His commitment inside Welsh people group effectively built up these social qualities, making an association that rose above sports and resounded with the more extensive populace.

Furthermore, the part features Williams' mentorship of youthful abilities, accentuating his job in sustaining the future. By sharing his encounters, bits of knowledge, and giving direction, he effectively added the improvement of hoping for competitors. Williams' mentorship turned into a type of local area commitment that went past monetary help, cultivating an inheritance that reaches out into the future through the people he enlivened.

In rundown, the section on local area commitment lays out a representation of JPR Williams as a figure profoundly put resources into having a beneficial outcome past individual accomplishments. His association in worthy missions, active local area administration, social impact, and mentorship on the whole exhibit a guarantee to adding to the prosperity of networks. Williams' heritage in local area commitment highlights the groundbreaking force of sports figures in

JPR Williams

encouraging positive change and leaving an enduring engraving on the networks they contact.

7.4 RETIREMENT

JPR Williams' retirement denotes the decision of a celebrated and effective part in rugby history, flagging the conclusion of an important time period that saw his athletic brightness, authority, and commitments to the game. The section on retirement investigates the subtleties of this change, revealing insight into how Williams explored the choice to pull back from the game and the resulting periods of his life.

The story unfurls the variables that impacted Williams' choice to resign from proficient rugby. Whether incited by the actual cost of the game, a longing to investigate new pursuits, or the acknowledgment that the time had come to elapse the light to the future, the section dives into the contemplations that formed this huge choice. Williams' retirement turns into a significant second, inciting reflection on the perfection of a recognized playing profession.

Williams' rugby involvement does not, however, end with his retirement. The story investigates how he progressed into jobs like training and tutoring, effectively adding to the advancement of the game. His ongoing involvement demonstrates a commitment to giving back and passing on the wealth of knowledge and experience he has gained throughout his illustrious career, ensuring that he will have a long-lasting impact on the rugby landscape.

Past rugby, the section on retirement enlightens how Williams diverted his energies and abilities. Whether heightening his interests in the clinical field, taking part in local area administration, or investigating other individual interests, retirement turns into a time of multi-layered tries. The story highlights a day to day

JPR Williams

existence past the rugby pitch, displaying Williams' versatility and flexibility as he explores new roads.

The narrative is intricately woven with the emotional aspects of retirement. The section investigates the blended sentiments, the wistfulness for the adrenaline of the game, and the satisfaction got from a lifelong that made a permanent imprint. Williams is able to reflect on his accomplishments, acknowledge the difficulties he has overcome, and embark on the next phase of his life with a sense of fulfillment and pride during his retirement.

The tradition of JPR Williams takes on new aspects in retirement. The section uncovers what his mean for go on through training, mentorship, and local area commitment. Williams' influence extends beyond the playing field, influencing the narrative of rugby and contributing to the well-being of society as a whole, so retirement is no longer an end point but rather a transition into a new phase.

JPR Williams

In rundown, the section on retirement paints a nuanced picture of JPR Williams as he explores the significant shift from dynamic playing to a diverse life past rugby. Retirement turns into a passage to new open doors, proceeded with commitments to the game, and a getting through inheritance that rises above the limits of his playing vocation.

7.5 REFLECTION

In the narrative of JPR Williams, the section titled "Reflections" provides a moving look at the reflective moments that occurred after his remarkable rugby and medical careers. This period of reflection gives a material to Williams to consider the highs, lows, and the horde encounters that formed his excursion. It turns into a story space where he distils the pith of his accomplishments, challenges, and the persevering through influence he abandons.

JPR Williams

Reflections on the rugby field include returning to notorious minutes, from victorious triumphs to the difficulties of wounds and misfortunes. The account dives into how these reflections act as standards for assessing self-improvement, versatility, and the commitment made to the game. Williams' thoughtfulness turns into a method for valuing the subtleties of his playing style, initiative characteristics, and the unyielding soul that characterized his presence on the rugby pitch.

The section investigates reflections on authority, particularly during his captaincy in the 1976 Five Countries Title. Williams' thought digs into the essential choices made, the difficulties confronted, and the effect of his initiative in group elements. This reflective phase provides an opportunity to distill lessons learned in the captaincy role and provide insights into leadership and resilience that go beyond rugby.

JPR Williams

Reflections on the clinical vocation exhibit a double story — triumphs, challenges, and the developing scene of sports medication. Williams' examination considers an appraisal of the effect he made in muscular health and the convergence of his clinical vocation with his rugby process. The part unfurls as a review investigation of the fragile harmony between two requesting and effective expert pursuits.

Close to home reflections become an essential part of this section, diving into the significant association Williams had with the game, the networks he served, and the persevering through social importance. The account catches snapshots of win, kinship with partners, and the close to home load of addressing Ridges and the English and Irish Lions. Williams' appearance typify the profound intricacy of a profession that goes past measurements, epitomizing the quintessence of enthusiasm and obligation to rugby.

The story of reflections likewise stretches out to life past the rugby pitch, investigating self-improvement, family,

JPR Williams

and the more extensive effect on society. Williams' thought on the inheritance he leaves turns into a strong part of this section. It features a man who not just succeeded in that frame of mind of sports and medication yet additionally added to the social texture of Grains, leaving an enduring effect on the networks he drew in with.

In rundown, the part on appearance in JPR Williams' story gives a profoundly thoughtful focal point through which he mulls over the multi-layered parts of his life. It turns into a story space for valuing accomplishments, refining illustrations, and recognizing the profound extravagance that characterized his excursion in rugby, medication, and local area commitment.

CONCLUSION

In Quest for Rugby Greatness" finishes up as a convincing story that typifies the unprecedented excursion of JPR Williams, winding around together the strings of wins, challenges, and the multi-layered inheritance he abandons. The story unfurls as a demonstration of a daily existence lived chasing greatness, on the rugby field as well as in the domains of medication, administration, and local area commitment.

The conclusion reflects Williams' unwavering dedication to the team's success, brave tackles, and strategic brilliance. It investigates the development of the fullback position under his impact, depicting him as a permanent pioneer blemish on the game's scene. Williams' rugby inheritance isn't restricted to insights yet is enhanced by the social importance he accomplished, turning into an image of Welsh pride and strength.

JPR Williams

Past the rugby pitch, the end dives into Williams' progress from dynamic play to retirement, featuring his proceeded with commitments through training, mentorship, and local area administration. Retirement turns into an entryway to new open doors, displaying his versatility and the getting through influence he stretches out into different features of life. The story investigates the close to home reverberation of reflections, offering a brief look into the contemplative minutes that follow a vocation loaded up with highs, lows, and significant associations.

The tradition of JPR Williams, as portrayed in the end, rises above the limits of sports and medication. It turns into a tradition of initiative, social impact, and a guarantee to having a beneficial outcome on the networks he drew in with. The story exemplifies a daily existence that, in quest for rugby magnificence, turned into a rich embroidery of encounters, values, and commitments that reverberate across ages.

JPR Williams

In rundown, "In Quest for Rugby Greatness" finishes up by laying out an exhaustive representation of JPR Williams as a figure whose impact stretches out a long ways past the attempt lines. The story praises his accomplishments, ponders the difficulties survive, and investigates the getting through inheritance he leaves — an inheritance set apart by greatness, flexibility, and a significant effect on the universe of rugby and then some.

Printed in Great Britain
by Amazon

62411e5a-416b-4144-bd7a-1ebed1104d71R01